It's This

Laura Foley

Fernwood
PRESS

It's This

©2023 Laura Foley

Fernwood Press
Newberg, Oregon
www.fernwoodpress.com

Printed in the United States of America

Cover and page design: Mareesa Fawver Moss

ISBN 978-1-59498-103-6

For Clara, Chloe and Lorca
Aaron, Sam and Evelyn
Billy, Larissa, Eleanor and Milo
Nina and Cory
And all the bees and butterflies

Table of Contents

Acknowledgments

Grateful acknowledgment is made to the editors of the journals and anthologies who first published the following poems. The poems, sometimes in earlier versions, appeared as follows:

After I Attend a Talk: *One Art*

An Ordinary Sunday: *Valparaiso Poetry Review*

Bad Catholic: *Live Encounters*

Breakfast Conversation: *One Art*

Breaking Free: *Buddhist Poetry Review*

Coastal Globe: *Live Encounters*

Debut and Finale: *Adanna*

Everything We Need: *Live Encounters*

Full Tide: *One Art*

If It Were Up to Me, We Would Eat Clouds for Dinner: *Live Encounters*

In New York Harbor: *Live Encounters*

It Matters: *One Art*

Let Me Be Worthy: *Agape Review*

Like Rain, Like Snow: *Live Encounters*

Looking the Other Way: *Amethyst Review*

Lost and Found: *Parks and Points*

Meditation in Ice: *Switchback Review*

Nine Ways of Looking at Light: *National Outermost Poetry Grand Prize Winner*

Not Hearing: *Mason Street*

Octubre: *Honorable Mention, Gemini Magazine Poetry Contest*

Of Thirty Thousand: *Naugatuck River Review*

O Lift Me as a Wave: Soul-Making Keats Award

On the Way: *Red Eft Review*

Radiance: *One Art Poetry*

Shadows and Light: *Poetry Society, London, Contest Winner*

Sieve: *Live Encounters*

Symbiosis: *Live Encounters*

Speaking Meadow: *Crannog Magazine, Ireland*

Swing: *Adelaide*

The Absent Place: *Valparaiso Poetry Review*

The Hill: *Atlanta Review*

The Meaning of the Dog Digging in the Grass: *Crannóg Magazine, Ireland*

The Mind of a Day: *Live Encounters*

Then: *One Art*

The Orchard on Its Way: *DMQ Review*

The Rising: *Amethyst Review*

To See It: *A Year of Being Here*

We Named Her Cumpleaños: *Muddy River Review*

Year End: *DMQ Review*

Introduction

The first poem in *It's This*, "The Rising," perfectly illustrates James Crews' praise of Laura Foley, "Her poems...can seem deceptively simple at first." The first three stanzas seem to offer an unmitigated appreciation of the sights, sounds, and touch of nature, "the symphony of wind...lifting my hair... a few white clouds / sailing the sky's blue sea," but the fourth stanza begins to suggest something more complex:

> "I wait as the gentle,
> unburning, low sun
> goldens the weary grass,
> the scattered fallen leaves."

The repetition of the "I wait" in the first stanza, here and in the final stanza, implies expectation and the exercise of patience or the management of impatience. The use of "gentle, unburning," acknowledges the sun's harmful potential, yet it "goldens the weary grass, / the scattered fallen leaves," making exhaustion, aging, and decay beautiful," suggesting the speaker's acceptance of the inevitable. The final, koan-like stanza seems to embrace paradox:

"I wait, but hear only the empty wind,

growing louder, echoing

the emptiness inside me,

rising to meet

the nothing I was seeking,"

but after all the waiting, the speaker hears "only empty wind," suggesting that something else was expected or sought, something which doesn't echo "the emptiness inside me." Yet the wind also rises "to meet / the nothing I was seeking," which suggests satisfaction and connection in that meeting, that echo, that oneness.

But to what does this "nothing" refer? To the meditation practice of clearing the mind of noise, busyness, competing thoughts, to letting go of attachments? It seems that the speaker accomplishes this—and yet the statement, "I wait, but," suggests otherwise, which implies that like a koan, the answer cannot be found in logic, but in acceptance, wisdom, belief or mystery—and perhaps in a state of being which need not wait, which simply is.

All of this is very much in conversation with Wallace Stevens' famous poem, "The Snow Man," whose speaker "listens" to wind, where "The Rising" "hears" wind and "waits." Stevens' sun is "distant," where Foley's is "gentle, unburning." Stevens' speaker, "nothing himself, beholds / Nothing that is not there and the nothing that is." Foley's hears "only the empty wind...echoing / the emptiness inside me, / rising to meet / the nothing I was seeking." Both poems explore paradox, and end with paradox, and lest you think any of this happened by accident, the subject of Foley's prize-winning master's thesis at Columbia University was Stevens' poetry. Her conversation with him may have been unconscious or begun unconsciously, but is a conversation nonetheless.

The final lines of "Breaking Fee: Zen Ordination" echo the first poem's koan-like acceptance of paradox, mystery, and the state of being which simply is:

> "breathing freely, you find your new self stuck in traffic,
> smiling and not smiling, in almost equal degree.

"The Rising" seems to accept mortality, but the second poem, "Intuition," both acknowledges death, and denies it. The speaker sees a deer skeleton by the roadside and doesn't stop to "wonder" or "ponder"; she drives "quickly by." In "Spring Treachery, her expectations / goals are undermined again, in being injured while walking in the woods:

> "taken down by a path I thought kind—
> a familiar wooded walk hiding its ice
> beneath a sheath of old dried leaves."

This, and the title "treachery," suggest that she blames nature, yet the first two lines, "I slip, grabbing twigs as I fall, / assaulting an innocent hemlock," accept blame for injuring nature—more deceptively simple nature poems, more complex paradox, and much to admire in Foley's poetry, which overall recalls Robert Frost more than Wallace Stevens, in his deceptively simple, completely accessible descriptions of nature, which may be successfully mined for complexity.

If It's This begins with denial and undermining of the speaker's hopes, goals, and growth, with a death and the awareness of mortality, it also moves very quickly to poems of transformation and change. In "Radiance," the speaker experiences an epiphany of belief, which begins the dissolution of her marriage, as she rejects her husband's "non-belief." In "Debut and Finale," she celebrates a same-sex lover who "who cherishes me / at my most exposed." In the next poem, "Octubre," she and her lesbian partner and their dogs have become "a family."

Poems celebrating their marriage and grandmotherhood follow, and are woven throughout the manuscript, connected by the speaker's gratitude and appreciation for all she has—and the knowledge that she will lose it. If "Death is the mother of beauty" (Stevens) in these poems, it's also the mother of appreciation and gratitude:

> "I have to turn away,
> to savor the love
> one of us will lose,
> our loneliest day."

The speaker learns to pay greater attention in her outdoor walking and sitting meditations, to "look / through the mind of a day," and savor its beauties:

> "...rain and sun bestowed by sky,
> on each leaf and tree,
> on the whole sea of living green,
> clouds massing and vanishing..."

and to "seek beyond the *No*" after the world "kicks you in the head / again and again" ("Then"),

> "so the healing bell inside yourself
> will resound, in quietness,
> with *Yes*
> and *Yes* and *Yes*."

In "Holiness," the speaker teaches her grandchildren this *Yes*, akin to the sacredness in nature of which John Muir wrote so much. He no doubt would have approved of teaching her granddaughter to meditate on a hilltop, and another day's goal to:

> "loose the ribbons of ourselves
> to the spirits of the wind."

In "Prayer," though the speaker prays to be given more daily beauties,

> "so we may learn
>
> to surrender
>
> all of it with grace,"

she's also asking herself to pay greater attention, and to practice gratitude, to be fully present in each moment, as so many of these poems, including the wonderful final poem, "Nine Ways of Looking at Light," suggests:

> "this precious slant of summer sun,
>
> clouds arriving to veil the light,
>
> a gentle voice of waves on stone,
>
> *It's this, it's this, it's this.*"

In a subtle and lovely bookend to "The Rising," the final section of this final poem ends with rising, and acceptance of change: of season, of mortality, of life stages, "this sip of coffee / over so quickly"—and paradox, in seeing and not seeing, but seeing clearly through a veil, the bardo that is life, between rebirth and death:

> "I walk this foggy dawn to see the seals,
>
> where they sleep beneath the scrim
>
> rain makes of rising light,
>
> to hear the music of their steady breath—
>
> a holy time before the changing of the tide."

I invite readers to brew a cup of coffee and sit near a window, to sip from it and *It's This*, to savor all that these deftly spare and vivid poems have to offer of peace, contentment, gratitude, and joy, with as much simplicity or complexity as they wish.

—April Ossmann,
author of *Event Boundaries* and *Anxious Music*

I

The Rising

I wait on the mountaintop,
hearing the symphony of wind
in leafless trees, lifting my hair,
rising from unseen streams,
canyons of air, the sound

like ocean surf, rising,
falling, rising again,
a few white clouds
sailing the sky's blue sea.

Two eagles rise over me,
wheeling infinity symbols
around each other.

I wait as the gentle,
unburning, low sun
goldens the weary grass,
the scattered fallen leaves.

I wait but hear only the empty wind,
growing louder, echoing
the emptiness inside me,
rising to meet
the nothing I was seeking.

Intuition

I saw a deer skeleton
gracing the roadside
and didn't stop to wonder
where the flesh had gone,
why just a tuft of fur clung,
a bit of tail.
Didn't pause to ponder
its change from leaping-warmth
to cold, clean bones.
Didn't stop but glimpsed
crisp, dark lines against snow,
rib cage, long legs, perfect spine—
what we with mounded dirt,
neat lawn, and flowered stones
seek so hard to hide—
I drove quickly by.

Spring Treachery

I slip, grabbing twigs as I fall,
assaulting an innocent hemlock—
skinning my palms, arms, legs,
landing muddy-bruised and sore,
taken down by a path I thought kind—
a familiar wooded walk hiding its ice
beneath a sheath of old, dried leaves.

Radiance

I remember when I stopped
not believing in God, it sent me
to my knees pleading,
hands clasped like a penitent
or a medieval saint transported
to the modern age,
struck by my mother's stroke.
A litany flowed through me
of faintly remembered prayers,
growing as I spoke,
my knees impervious to hard tile,
cramped between sink and bath.
Yet, when I opened the door,
I feigned no inner change,
knew my husband's unknowingness
would try to eclipse my newfound light,
turn brilliance to a dull watered gray
with his dismissive gaze, the planet
of his non-belief
blocking me from radiating.
I didn't wish to rejoin him in the cave
where I once found comfort,
watching shadows dance.
It was the start
of the end of us, the beginning
of my brighter epoch.

Why She Would Get Up
to Go Look in the Mirror

It wasn't the blue-green-hazel
of her eyes she hadn't noticed
since her teens—nor shape
of face, color of hair,
not what she looked like
to others. Something else
compelled her
to leave her seat
in the middle of history class,
to find the restroom mirror,
to greet those wide-awake eyes
and new-found smile—
the friend who, at forty-five,
had just arrived.

Breaking Free: Zen Ordination

If you are free of illusion, life is worthwhile
and not worthwhile to an almost equal degree.
        —Carl Jung

At attention on your zafu every dawn, legs crossed,
spine straight to avoid patrolling monks' sharp prods.
Eat in unison, clean your bowl, crease your napkin in a six-point fold.
Sew your robe till midnight, record in neatest penmanship
the lineage from Buddha through Roshi to you,
accept the incense, prostrations, chanting,
the new name given to you, bending your head
to Roshi's feet. Driving home after two weeks,
breathing freely, you find your new self stuck in traffic,
smiling and not smiling in almost equal degree.

For Thirty-Three Points

Playing Scrabble with my lover,
I'm down a game—no vowels—
but I've got a *Q. Please God—*
I hear the words leak out of me—
Give me an I, and it's too late
to take it back, a wasted supplication,
but *He* guides my fingers darkly
through the velvet sack.

Debut and Finale

As I strolled beachward
through an alley of palms,
he filmed me from behind,
over and over, in over-lapping
fugue-like sequences,
to match Scarlatti's counterpoint,
then close-up, curled,
lying on a sandy dune,
my nude acting debut, and finale,
shown at the Whitney.
Why remember this now,
walking a drizzly waterfront,
soft spring rain
tapping our cheeks
like ghostly fingers—
him so long gone,
replaced at last
by a lover who matches me
in age, complexion,
gender, temperament,
who cherishes me
at my most exposed.

Octubre

If you saw me driving in this pelting rain,
you'd never guess my errand—
to buy lilies
for my butterfly.
He'll savor the flowers' aroma
this cold November day,
since wild blooms
have faded away.
Octubre lives in a screened-in cage
because I couldn't let him out
in last week's snow, could I?
He seems content, his feet sticky
against the screen, pleased to drink
when I uncurl his proboscis
with a toothpick, dip it
in honey water while he sucks
through his trunk-like tongue.
I say *he* because he has two spots
like eyes, on his hind side,
that indicate *boy*—
good for our family
of two lesbians, two bitches
(a Shepherd and a Lab),
and thirty thousand girl bees
who spent the whole autumn
dragging the hairy drones
out of the hive, killing them,
dumping the corpses
in a heap out front.

I'm just saying, it's good to have
some masculine energy 'round here,
even if it's just one Monarch
who hangs upside-down all day
and sometimes flutters his gorgeous wings.

Lost and Found

On my sophomore science field trip
to the rocky Massachusetts coast,
I sat captivated by a tidal pool, a little village
of crawling crabs, snails, starfish darting,
a sea anemone appearing to sing.
I stayed so long I forgot the rising tide,
my teachers, classmates waiting
on the bus. On the exam,
I couldn't calculate the pitch of waves
or chemical composition of anything,
but I knew how to lose myself
in the world of tiny shifting things.

To See It

We need to separate
to see the life we've made,
to leave our house
where someone waits, patiently,
warm beneath the sheets,
to don layers of armor,
sweater, coat, mittens, scarf,
to stride down the frozen road,
putting distance between us
this cold winter morning,
to look back and see,
on the hilltop, our life,
lit from inside.

Blood in the Snow

A glimpse of gray-brown fur—
large doe bounding into the woods—her mate's
blood steaming against ice. Boot tracks,
signs of dragging a heavy carcass through snow.

Not legal to shoot so near the road,
but no one to see the hunter step around the children's sled,
propped against a pine, so near the house.

We mourn the buck's passing and the widowing,
the doe who stayed, as a human might,
at the place her mate was taken, before leaving,
to live alone beneath snow-heavy limbs.

Then

The human world
kicks you in the head
again and again—

so you must seek beyond the *No*,
the song of dried beech leaves
ringing in the brittle wind,

a hollow tone to shiver you
like a tuning fork,
so the healing bell inside yourself

will resound, in quietness,
with *Yes*
and *Yes* and *Yes*.

Full Tide

We walked downhill
to the beach, her hand in mine,
small step after small step.
She said *Hi* to the *doggie* on the leash,
Hi Mommy to a woman passing
on the street, *Hi Daddy* to a bearded man.
On the sand, she stared transfixed
at the water, the slight waves,
the tide not yet pulling out.
She looked up toward a flap of wings.
Bird, I said, pointing at the seagull,
and she mimicked, *Bird,*
then turned her gaze back
to the waves' slow slapping.
Later I sat, looking at trees below me,
a hint of haze burning off the far bay,
the world busy working and sailing,
waking, while I sat waiting as Evie napped
that quiet Maine morning,
the full tide of grandmotherhood
lapping my shore.

The Orchard on Its Way

I wish it would slow,
not the train but the ponies,
shivering in a rain-soaked pasture,
a hundred geese fluttering
in a soggy field,
the eagles' wild mating dance
we saw this morning
from a Vermont station—
not the train but the passing
into memory—I want it all
to last, the chimney falling
back to bricks,
the orchard on its way to bud,
the kiss you gave me
twenty miles back.

The Absent Place

Her husband rests
in the slanting Adirondack chair,
centered on the lawn he's just cut
for the first time this summer—
the one they know is her last,
though she's not yet sixty.
He savors the fragrant spice
of shorn grass and blooming lavender,
forgetting, for a moment,
her tumors' malignant flowering.
She heats water in a copper pot,
stirs in sugar, simmers
hummingbird nectar
as the tiny whirring birds arrive:
one, then two, then one again,
hovering in the absent place
where the feeder once hung.

Not Hearing

A dog shifts soundlessly
at my feet beneath the table
where I sit, not writing.

Raindrops fall slow-motion
on neon grass,
on the hill of snow receding—

the longest, slowest winter,
dissolving into memory
like an uneasy dream

on waking—as peonies
thrust through soil
with their fountain pen heads.

Though my pen moves,
I am not writing,
not believing,

not hearing the symphony
of spring's instruments,
not hearing my breath

for the flood of unwritable words,
as the second dog
shifts her weight,

quickening sound
of legs in motion,
running in place.

Breakfast Conversation

I've placed her favorites—
fresh raspberries, string cheese,
a glass of milk in the giraffe cup—
on her highchair tray.
As she munches away,
swinging her short legs,
she asks thoughtfully,
Grandma, are you
pooping?
I continue my bite of oatmeal,
take a sip of coffee,
respond—*No darling.*
How about you?
She isn't either—
as we both wonder
what to say next.

Crickets

on
lawn
edges
in autumn
presage
long
cold
nights
spent
eye
to eye
with
snow's
cozy
hush I no
longer
hear
thanks
to those
chirping
in
my
ears.

Let Me Be Worthy

Of our sun-glazed hill's
snow-bright sanctuary,
the indoor fig tree
we tend together, growing
tender new leaves,
our companionable,
silent morning reading,
my unselfconscious walk
in bathrobe and cleats
down the steep hill
in crisp winter air,
claiming it—*yes, bliss,*
an answer to prayers
murmured for years,
including last night.

Ode to a Wasp

You dove into my hot chai—
I'm sorry you died,
though at least it was brief
and cinnamon-sweet.
I wonder if I
will be so blessed.

II.

Meditation in Ice

Prisms of frozen light,
this field of snow where I sit

and think until thoughts
that cloud the heart thin into nothingness,

revealing blue sky underneath—
and in that emptiness, tenderness rises

for my special-needs daughter,
may she find someone to love her as much as I do—

my daughter, who would appreciate
these gleaming ice flecks on top of snow's hard crust

formed by last week's thaw and refreezing
into fantastic shapes, reflecting the setting sun—

beauty children anywhere would see more quickly
than the rest of us, caged children separated

from immigrant parents, hungry children
in rusting trailers in the hills around my small town,

homeless children in cities, children of privilege,
beauty anyone could see if they looked appreciatively,

prisms made by ice and light—
a day-lit half moon etched against the blue,

a globe of sky over the globe of Earth,
tilting on its axis away from sun and back,

over this field of snow, where I sit alone
on a hilltop, until I think of nothing

but light—light on snow, light
prisming ice, light on light on light.

In New York Harbor

Though Catholic,
my father chose fire,
his ashes dispersed in saltwater—
no grave, no bones, no body
to lie beside his mother and father.

As the tide drove us seaward,
I didn't expect the plunge
into darkness—the shadow
of the monumental statue,
a she-god rising over waves—

nor the motion of the silent craft,
engine stopped, cross-currents
pulling us back through ashes,
as if we or they were a sieve—
sure I heard his laughter.

The Hill

It rises above our house like a sentinel,
shepherding sapling trees, and it occurs to me
we could cut and stack some, let them dry
in the barn we don't yet have
for the animals we don't yet own,
but I imagine the hill is willing to host
fantasy or reality, chickens for sure,
because of the eggs, goats,
and maybe a lamb,
because she loves them.
We'll burn the wood
in fires I'll build in our fireplace
as we toast with hot chocolate—
the hill protecting us
from winter's coldest winds.
She'll wear a helmet and leg protectors,
cut the thinner maples and birch,
as together we clear a gradual,
rocky path up the greatest slope.
We'll get married this summer on the lawn—
not hers but ours, our farm
with chickens, goats, a barn—
the steep path rising above the house,
allowing a heavenly view hidden from us
as we go about the business of living
but revealed each time we climb
to the summit for the perspective
of someone watching over us.

Year End

I want to bury him,
though I doubt it's appropriate
for a butterfly.
Perhaps I'll climb the icy hill,
trudge through woods and slippery snow
to place him as close as I can to sky
in the field he would have floated over
on his way to Mexico
if October hadn't been too cold for flight.
The orange-and-black-winged beauty
thrived in his screened-in cage
lit with purple happy lights
and fed every day by hand,
his proboscis dipped in honey water,
until, on Christmas day,
he birthed three sacs of sperm,
a rare gift for me these days.
Finding no mate,
he folded his wings and died,
face pressed into the New Year's daisy
I gave him as a human lover might.

Summer Day

Here floats the mind on summer's dock,
on a sluggishness that waves any anxiety away—
long lines of verse river the page
in mimicry of sun's most generous days,
and crows caw lazily from thick-leafed limbs
like rum-dazed sailors floating on a tranquil sea.
Hazy clouds wisp and don't quite form to shapes,
thinning to mist baked to nothing,
the sun claiming lordship over creation.
Only minnows in the cooler darkness of a shaded pool
dart, circle restlessly, in an eddying stream
made low by heat and lack of rain.
The dash of water on a rock is but a whisper
lulling listeners to sleep, to dream of being.

After I Attend a Talk
by the Somali Refugee

Migrating south for my annual holiday,
I'm at ease on the bus to the ferry,
where I will cross a wide bay,
relax at the sea.
Wheels rumble beneath me,
landscapes unfold
like a dream of plenty—
yellow lilies in a field,
gardens rich with eggplants,
tomatoes, raspberries,
reminding me of home,
where my love,
a woman to whom I'm legally married,
awaits my return.
Soon I will breathe salt sea air,
while winds from another continent
ruffle my hair like one beloved,
as I delight in ocean surf,
gulls' raucous calling,
the freedom of movement
others die for.

Of Thirty Thousand

I look into the hive
to greet my bees
after the long winter freeze
and see them—caught—

in media res,
heads burrowed
in their own sweetness,
their house turned tomb.

I admire their industry,
all they did in the months
since I last looked in—
the reproducing, the honey-making

that kept them alive
until some moment after
I heard them buzzing
and busy last week.

The hive is silent
as Pompeii after the ash,
but not post-lava or earthquake,
just northern cold's too-long, silent grip.

I poke with a stick,
wish for one to rise and whirr
its golden-striped body
in new spring sun.

Just one.
But none.

On the Way

A soft spring morning,
tender rain after a violent night
of house-shaking winds,
loud belts of thunder.
As I stride to my car
with backpack,
yoga mat, snacks,
my wife calls to me
from our bedroom's
second-floor window—
she must have removed the screen—
she leans out,
calling in love and friendliness,
and it occurs to me
I finally have what I wanted
all my life, as I smile back
on the way to my day.

Alternative Reality

The two-year-old resists my hand,
walks on her own down the steep drive,
kicks a lump of snow she calls, *rock*.
At the bottom of the hill, Christmas
waits in sacks, bright wrapper and ribbon
just visible through black plastic, cardboard
waving from the recycling bin in December wind.
A truck rumbles up just in time for us, and she calls
happily to *Santa Claus*, who jumps out and waves back
as he loads the trash into his noisy sleigh.
In white beard, ski cap, fluorescent green vest,
I can see what she has seen in him
and how he now begins to see himself
as he *Ho-Ho-Ho's* down the road,
red tail-lights twinkling, engine thundering
as he grinds the gears like a hundred reindeer.

Bad Catholic

I'm waiting
my turn for the dark
confession booth
remembering
to cross myself
      right hand
to forehead
      center
left
      right
don't mix it up

I'm gabbling
blessmefatherforIhavesinned
I'm fibbing
Idisobeyedmymother
toldonmysister
hoping to
dispose quickly of three *Hail Marys*
two *Our Fathers*—

before I can escape
to October's grace
      a crisp fall day
made for running
in new shoes
      of heavenly blue.

In Poetry Group

Late October hosts the thin time,
veils between worlds translucent,
our group host beatific as we read a poem
by a long-gone poet about an artichoke—
when the lights flicker off and the heavy
basement door swings wide—opening
on a darker darkness below us, as Deb screams,
and the hairs stand up on all our necks.

We haven't been together as a group
since our poet friend, Blair, died,
and who knows, maybe he doesn't like
the poem about artichokes, or maybe he misses us
as we miss him, as the door slowly shuts
with no visible hand returning it to stasis.

We Named Her *Cumpleaños*

She cocooned on my birthday, spinning wildly all day,
then hung like a stilled green bell from a leaf stem
I had placed in the open jug we called her home.

Ten days on, her covering turned translucent black,
giving a window view of her wings'
black and orange beauty.

Then, as we held our breath, some unnamed energy
seemed to leave, stopping the progress of change,
as if the thought of opening became too much to bear.

Still cocooned weeks past her time, my fool's hope
chose to lay her gently on the ground
under the raspberry bush, well past the time of ripe berries,

but no god rose from her shroud,
and I wished to think no more of her or birthdays
and what they signify.

Still, I kept wondering, as the days shortened,
if I'd somehow wronged her
in trying to direct her metamorphosis,

as winter barged in with its egotistical force,
its snow and wind burying
the shell from whence a soul had fled.

Imagine

Just before my Christmas company
drove over the hills toward Maine,
as my toddler companion and I
approached my home, I glimpsed
in an upstairs window her mom
and dad, waving down at us.

I crouched next to my kin,
pointing until she saw, too. Imagine
seeing your reason for being,
framed, like a photograph,
waving and smiling at you.

I scooped her in my arms,
and we rushed inside, so she could hug
her favorite people in the world,
and I could brace myself
for the next goodbye.

It Matters

that Mary Oliver *woke early*
and walked along the bay, as morning sun
tore the sheets of darkness from the sky.
It matters that she carried a notebook
and cared to look into a kingfisher's soul,
to dig in wet sand for clams
in which she later tasted the salt sea
erupting in her mouth like sex—
that she *let the soft body of her body love*
what it loved, which was Molly.
It matters that she loved a woman.
It matters that we each wake
to stride our own snow dunes,
finding in each day something of value,
even the last ash leaf hanging on a winter limb,
shivering a bit, then falling into stillness,
over and over to lose ourselves
into something larger,
something better. It matters that I clutch
my stack of her books—those fields of light—
now that her body has gone
into *the cottage of darkness.*

Speaking Meadow

Above the hermit thrush's flute-like
rush of descending minor notes,
in a high field where butterflies sip from clover,
golden rod sways on stems
grown longer than thought could make them,
where oats grow even taller, where two dogs,
tired from a steep hike, sleep in soft grass,
where a breeze arises, ruffles the leaves,
where time has aged the barley from luscious green
to delicate, dry beige, a human's come
to feel the day's change, from sun-slant morning
to wide spread of midday heat,
to rest above the world of naming,
among the no less articulate meadows,
birds, insects, stones, flowers.

Marriage

We live much of our days
in separate places.

I tap maples and boil sap
while she bakes.

We pour my hot gold
over her oven-warm cakes

and taste, each in our place,
the sweetness we've made.

Everything We Need

I take my granddaughter to the beach,
a frigid Maine inlet,
but it's hot enough, this summer day,
that the cold dark deep will feel
tingly-good against skin.

Dipping one sandaled toe in,
she exclaims to gulls, to the sea,
and me, to twelve bored geese
floating offshore: *I'm swimming!*
I quibble, *Not exactly, Dear.*

Acclimating, she wades in
ankle-deep, swirls hands
in the gray-green surface
of everything we need to survive.
Look! I'm swimming like a butterfly.

Yes, darling, I surrender,
then swing her, as she giggles,
kicking legs making
a foaming white wake,
as we engine through the sea together.

Passing Glance

When they die,
the departed cast a passing glance
at those they loved, a figurative nod,
ending in spectral wishing well,
before leaving for eternity,
as we live on and on,
attached to the day, the time,
the place of their last breath.
A day in May returns,
fifteen years later,
as I relive hours spent in vigil,
hard decisions,
the burial of a being already flown
beyond the mortal cycle of years.

An Ordinary Sunday

On Sunday, I sing in a church choir, not believing
in God but holding a space for something—

some might call it spirit, an opening,
a candle illuminating a cave.

On Sunday, I climb the hill behind our house,
as the long winter thaws, and my dogs dig in wet loam.

I wait for worries to relax their hold, for my mind
to become one with the clouds' calm drifting,

the trilling of a stream rushing somewhere unseen.
We need, I think, to let ourselves soften around hurt

before we melt, like spring snow, into fields—
so, I let Dad in, decades past his death,

find a few good memories, like stones just soft enough
for polishing—him filling the green glass vaporizer nightly,

so I wouldn't get sick, in my childhood winters' hot, dry air;
Dad donning an apron to cook for his skinny teen.

I breathe in the care and nourishment he offered then,
and I receive today, on an ordinary Sunday.

III.

Sieve

In a circle of birch trees,
in speckled morning light,
in summer's waning days,
beneath the unseen moon,
whose benevolence she feels
like a maternal spirit
guiding her tides,

in the stillness of a forest
high above the silent valley,
a radiating face emerges
among long, green grasses,
in the play of ening shadows,

a portal to the vast unknown,
beckoning a quiet human
with her wise canine friend
to enter in.

The forest whispers
of listening
to trees' breathing,
matching hers
to crickets' thrumming,
to leaves' swaying
in the softest
morning breeze,

releasing tension, fear,
trusting the woods' spirit

to carry her
everywhere she needs to be,
in peace, as morning light
dapples equally,
golden leaves sieved
by every cricket's violin.

Like Rain, Like Snow

The white pine weeps needles
leached of green—auburn snowflakes
I carry on shoulders and hair unaware
into palliative care, handing newspapers
to patients—as I lean, one plucks
a needle from my shoulder as wind
sifts the remainder from trees
like rain, like snow, drifting and burying.

Legacy

From their own bodies, the bees
made circles of wax, capping honey.
Living all year in the hive I gave them,
kept safe from bears by my electric fence,
they seemed happy, collecting nectar
from millions of flowers, feeding their queen,
killing unnecessary drones.
They died over the long snowy winter,
but left behind a treasure of honey,
this gold dollop I drop in my tea.
When I go,
I hope to leave something as sweet.

A Kind of Knowing

Perhaps love is a fritillary
butterfly sipping
nectar from clover
on this, my chosen love's
birthday. Perhaps love
is just this sitting,
this knowing she
breathes in our
home below,
thinking perhaps of me
on my hilltop seat,
far in yards but feeling
the cord of connection,
like the butterfly
fluttering across
wide waters to Mexico,
knowing where to go.

Symbiosis

Evelyn and I
climb the hill
in crisp sunrise.
I lift an oak leaf from the ground,
crusted with first frost
she touches, like fairy dust,
and pockets to show her dad.
We rest at a picnic spot
on wooden chairs,
close our eyes in meditation.
Listen, I say, *to the sounds*
you hear with closed eyes:
fallen leaves crinkling
in autumn's morning breeze,
blackbirds squawking, unseen,
somewhere in the high pines,
wind shuffling through hemlocks—
and, she asserts, in her thin,
high toddler voice, clear and glad
as a cardinal's trilling,
the chairs, listen to the chairs—
and we do, side by side,
with eyes closed,
instructing each other.

If It Were up to Me,
We'd Eat Clouds for Dinner

When my lovely wife
gets too deep into the weeds

of her wonderful cooking—
with paprika or cumin,

sautéed eggplant, cilantro,
braised carrots—my mind

drifts to the sky behind her—
clouds building an ark,

animals climbing aboard—
when I realize

she's waiting for a reply,
I pull my mind back

from the ibexes,
the skinny crocodile

merging with the fat unicorn—
I agree, *fried*

(or, wait, is it baked?)
would be great.

The Mind of a Day

When you sit looking from a porch
through the mind of a day,
you see rain and sun bestowed by sky
on each leaf and tree,
on the whole sea of living green,
clouds massing and vanishing,
breezes winging the scent
of freshly ripe lilacs,
neon-green grass blades
not yet cut this season.
You hear raindrops begin again,
each one separate from the other,
as a sky turns silver-gray,
radiant circles of light
growing in a rain puddle,
as a wind rises, rustling your hair,
equally as new-budding leaves—
the maple over your head,
elm cathedraling the street,
the whole village haloed
by woods—so much to see,
when everything else falls away,
and you're free to look
through the mind of a day.

Transmigration

This morning, it was new snow,

        soft as goose down, layered on frozen depths,

then, sitting by a window, watching chickadees' dipping flights—

        one, then another, landing lightly at the feeder.

Then, shoveling white fluff light as wings

        to forge a path to the driveway landing.

Then, sledding down our steep drive—

        swooshing around the hairpin curve.

Then, a weak sun peeking through gray

        like a blooming flower.

Last January, I placed the butterfly's open-winged body on a stone

        between two cut-leaf daisies—

but when I checked that night, body and soul were gone.

        Say he went into the stomach of a living bird,

say this cardinal, hopping and taking off—

        I think it's just right, don't you?

Turned into the flutter of bright red wings.

Wind Dowse

After a settling of mind
like whirling leaves
woven into forest floor,
you start to hear it,
sitting in stillness,
in thick, untrod snow,
the whispering zephyr
on one side, breeze
on the other, a sigh
behind, one waft crossing
the leafless valley,
you, breathing on the hilltop
in silence, long enough
and awake enough
to notice the difference.

Like Being a Child Again, Only Better

We walk at her pace—
she bends to pick up a leaf
on a quiet street, plops down to watch it
slowly crumble between her thumbs.
At the pebbled beach,
she finds rocks to climb,
jumps frog-like from one to another
as I hover. We make a driftwood house,
and she sits me beneath a bent
and wizened oak branch,
on a round stump, and serves me tea,
then makes ducklings out of stones, then
a fire truck, *vroom, vroom,*
swish, swish as she douses me
with pretend water. At naptime,
she goes instantly to sleep,
and I lie down, too, to think of her
and feel the soft Maine sun, still glowing
on my face—or maybe
my sense of her, glowing through me.
When we go out again,
she eats chickpeas from a bag,
announcing it to a stranger on his lawn,
showing him her dress adorned with stars,
confident in his interest and approbation.
We stroll along a boardwalk,
over a tidal river, and I point to a seal,
its whiskered head so clear above water,
she wonders, aloud, if it's Andre?

We walk slowly as evening curves over us,
as if we have all the time we need in the world,
and everything in my life has already happened.

Winter Morning

This calm, this new snow with layers of crisp ice
I crunch with every planting of cleated boot,
inscribing alleys of thick maple and birch,
black and white stripes of shade and gleam,
chickadees, blue jays, calling in the dawn
as light crests leaf-vacant hills,
illuminates neat fox-prints in the snow,
spreads warm fingers over an upturned human face
on the cusp of old age—
a Sunday morning above the intimate valley,
receiving the grace of this new day's sun.

Oh lift me as a wave, a leaf, a cloud!

I describe what I see outside her window,
a perspective, alien perhaps, to hers—
yellow and green leaves buffeted by winds,
white bark streaked with autumn sun.
It seems important to tell her the news
beyond her ICU cubicle, since she is hampered
by intubation, from the uplifting scene beyond
the squawking TV's obsession with everything dire.
The birches shimmer like bashful girls,
a few bright leaves dropping like lost invitations,
some landing in the gutter, some taking flight.

Looking the Other Way

I go out and climb the hill to see the way grass
accepts the wind's direction, how it yellows
with the season, goldenrod fading to ashy gray,
to brush my hair with the breeze, to hear
the poplar's leaves speaking of autumn's in-between.
But sometimes, instead of gazing at the woods I've climbed,
I turn and look the other way, toward mountains
that lead to other mountains and then the sea.
I imagine I'm a butterfly, the orange and black one
just now taking flight, lifting to the topmost branch.
I envision a thousand-mile journey along the coast,
over the Gulf's wide, churning waters,
her fragile escape. Then, from what I've gleaned
in contemplation of another's freedom, I'm ready
to descend, to accept the work of home again.

Shadows and Light

After a night of rain,
a puddle remains
cupped in stone,

as my bra cups
my breast—
shadowed perhaps,

as the little lake
is sunlit—
an eye gazing at me

with encouragement
or irony
I can't translate

as I await
the MRI's judgment.

Keeping Watch

Tonight, the fog of stars delineates to beacons
clearer than we have ever seen,
a starlight bright enough to light the garden path
to our bed this night, sailing on our backs
while our earthen ship tilts under us,
as if to capsize us into the sky.
A firefly arrives
between ourselves and greater lights,
strobing in hopes of attracting a mate
before its brief green light burns out.
We hold hands between sleeping bags,
watching as long as we can—
another blink or two in eternity's eye.

The Meaning of the Dog
Digging in the Grass

Same as the hill quiet with dark green pines,
the air rent by a crow's screeching,
the woodpecker's tap-tap-tapping into a hollowed tree,

same as the green clover sprig rising from a new-mown field,
a purple flower emerging after autumn frost,
feathers of milkweed seeds releasing into flight,

same as a poplar tree's silver shimmering in wind—
the cloud come to cool the skin of a human,
sitting cross-legged on the grass, breathing oneness in.

Fuel

Paddling Umbagog Lake, from New Hampshire
to Maine and back, cooking over open fires,
waking to moon lighting the lake at 3 a.m.,
sunrise paddle on glass-still water,
mist rising like a dream of Eden I imagined
we'd lose in the long drive home
or time rushing after; but we placed ourselves
in beauty's way, and it stays in our marrows,
fuel we use to warm long winter nights.

Swing

While the giddy bird feeder
swings over crusted snow,
Clara waters geraniums,
pots of rosemary, thyme,
a lemon tree. *Come, she says,*
smell the lemon tree, so sweet,
like Spain in spring, see
the fig, it grows new leaves
as if it doesn't know
we've got three feet of snow,
four months of winter left.
I bend to the replete
yellow buds she proffers,
then pivot, focusing
on yellow finches, as if
their golden fluttering
might gild me.
I have to turn away,
to savor the love
one of us will lose,
our loneliest day.

Holiness

I would leave the uncivil world
to its clamoring bad news,
focus on tending
the children of my children
from my rural perch,
teach them the liquid notes
of evening thrush,
savor honey from our beehives,
maple syrup from our trees,
take their hands and climb
the steep path behind the house,
picnic with a view
of circling blue hills,
loose the ribbons of ourselves
to the spirits of the wind.

Prayer

Give us this morning of wet grass,
of geese landing over us,
feet dangling as they drop
to the rippling pond.
Give us this bowl of mung beans,
these olives from Spain,
this garlic and kale—nourish us,
so we may be worthy,
this quiet May morning,
so we may learn
to surrender
all of it with grace.

Nine Ways of Looking at Light

I.

We moved the bed,
so the head faces north,
a wisdom we read
from India.
We dislodged a ghost,
her husband,
who, on these sheets,
some years ago expired.
We altered the angle
of our repose
and sleep all night
at peace, entwined.
We wake to morning hills,
trees, a great expanse,
a gentle, dappled light
new to us.

II.

The patient avoids the hospital window's view,
turning from snow's glare and stripped
winter trees, focusing on photos of dogs,
children, his hunting awards taped to the wall,
all invoking home, where he'd prefer to be,
this large man, with his bright white beard,
who doesn't read much, doesn't pray—
except now, with me, both of us shy,
until his eyes tear—
and his body shines from inside.

III.

No dappling leaves
but enough snow
on near branches now
to illuminate our window,
winter light grown greater
with snow's reflection.

IV.

We begin it with experiment,
hurling boiling water
to the frozen air,

watching it glitter
like glass confetti
crackling in the new year—

an answered wish
in every shining shard.

V.

Cold wind whips snow
so it swirls around our tallest pine,
a halo of light circling
a frigid angel or ghost
from my or someone else's past
seeking company
or just floating in the crisp winter air
for the wonder of it.

VI.

Not brown, not rust, but inexplicably white as bones,
these remnants dry as dust recall life, crackling,
as wind shivers them in barren early spring—
not one bud yet gracing it,
white leaves clung through snow and ice,
to shine and tremble in this Sunday light.

VII.

The dog shivers,
wet from a late spring swim,
whimpers as the wind
pulls light from the pond,
and we sit in shadows
by the water she knows,
just last summer, shone gold.

VIII.

This sip of coffee
over so quickly,
this guiding lighthouse
in the mist-less harbor,
moments before
the season changes,
this slip of wind along the bay,
a sweater saving me from chill,
this precious slant of summer sun,
clouds arriving to veil the light,
a gentle voice of waves on stone,
It's this, it's this, it's this.

IX.

I walk this foggy dawn to see the seals,
where they sleep beneath the scrim
rain makes of rising light,
to hear the music of their steady breath—
a holy time before the changing of the tide.

Thanks

Thanks so much to the Wednesday Poets—Sarah Snyder, Peg Brightman, Deb Franzoni, Jon Escher, Jill Herrick Lee, Lynne Byler, Brooke Herter James, Pam Ahlen; and to the River Poets—Sue Burton, Clyde Watson, Carol Westberg, Anne Shivas, Pam Harrison; for offering listening ears, critical guidance and companionship through the solitary process of creation. Thank you to workshop leaders Ellen Bass, Marie Howe, Kim Addonizio, Rick Barot, for your dedication to the art of poetry and generosity of instruction. Thank you to Billy Collins for creating The Cool People, The Night People, with bi-weekly broadcasts inspiring and instructing us, during COVID and beyond. Thank you Eric Muhr and Fernwood Press for birthing *It's This*, launching it beautifully into the world.

Title Index

First Line Index

A

E

F

G

H

I

J

L

M

9781594981036